Practical Stoicism

Ancient Philosophy for Modern Life

Your Step-By-Step Guide to Create A life of wisdom, perseverance and Joy

Nicholas Mayor

Contents:

Introduction

If your emotions control you, then everything else in the world can. Your ability to control your emotions and how they impact your decision-making determines how in control you are of your life.

You have to understand that you live in a chaotic world. There are so many things out there that are simply beyond your control. There are forces of nature that you really cannot predict, much less dispel. In fact, misfortunes happen every single day.

Given this reality, it should not be a surprise that, for almost all of us, we won't get everything that we want. That's just not going to happen. It may seem like we get what we're looking for from time to time, but in the big scheme of things, we can't control everything. We are bound for disappointment if we disregard this reality.

Unfortunately, if you have a tough time controlling your emotions, you will be disappointed again and again and again. If you let yourself be overcome by anger and frustration over the stuff that you really cannot control, your life will soon spiral out of control.

In fact, if you are feeling frustrated or you lack contentment at some level or another, it may be because of this. It may be because of the fact that you're trying to assert control over the things that you ultimately cannot control.

Bad stuff happens all the time. There are bad people out there. There are situations that we simply cannot control. The sooner we accept all of this, the better off we will all be.

Stoicism is simply a tool. That's all it is. It is a mental tool that will enable you to keep your emotions on track. This leads to greater self control, and this leads to the ability to overcome even the worst disappointments and disasters that life can bring our way.

It really all boils down to taking ownership of your internal, mental, psychological and emotional reality. If these things are lined up properly, regardless of what happens outside of you, you will still land on your feet. They will not impact you to the extent that you lose control and you live a life of misery and pain.

Chapter 1: What is Stoicism?

Stoicism is an ancient Greek school of philosophy. It originated in the city-state of Athens.

Founded by Zeno from the city-state of Citium, stoicism can be traced back to the early 3rd century BC. This is in the middle of the Hellenistic period of Western European history.

This school has quite a long list of illustrious Greek and Roman adherents. Some of the most famous stoics in history are the philosopher Epictitus, Seneca the great orator, and the Roman Emperor Marcus Aurelius.

Stoicism was the de facto philosophy of much of the upper classes of classical antiquity up until the middle of the Roman period.

What do Stoics Believe?

Stoics believe that virtue is the only thing that is good for human beings. You have to act with virtue.

Now, virtue cannot be applied to the natural world. It cannot be applied to animals, it cannot be applied to natural forces, and it definitely cannot be applied to greater historical and sociological forces. Instead, stoicism is very local in the sense that it locates virtue in every single human being.

Everybody can choose to be virtuous or not. They always have that choice, and it is very local. It is very personal. Understanding this then enables people to take control over their lives.

External realities, like how much money you have, how pleasurable your life is, how much comfort you enjoy, are not really good or bad. They're neutral. Instead, our virtue, or lack thereof, turn these things into positive or negative things.

In other words, the greater reality that confronts us day to day is essentially neutral.

What gives this neutral reality meaning is our exercise of virtue.

Either reality can be this oppressive day to day humiliation that drags us down, holds us back and makes us feel miserable, or it can be a daily celebration of our potential. It can be a daily reminder of the fact that we can create our reality and we can pursue our better angels to live life to our highest potential. It all boils down to choice, and this is contained in the concept of virtue.

Stoicism is built on the foundational assumption that the world, in and of itself, is unpredictable. The only thing that we can control is how we react to this unpredictability. That's the only thing that we can control. Our reactions or our responses to events that happen to us depends on our virtue.

Stoicism teaches people to practice the ability to respond to greater outside stimuli in a virtuous way. It teaches us to focus on the things that we can control and let go of the things that are beyond our control. That is the best we can do.

And the more we master the art of local control over ourselves, our emotions, our responses, the greater our competence becomes. This increased competence enables us to widen our circle of control and influence. It all begins with an awareness of this control over our responses to what the world brings on a moment by moment basis.

Not surprisingly, stoicism is all about living and enjoying the present moment. Instead of beating yourself up over things that happened in the past, you focus on what's in front of you. You focus on what's going through your head right here, right now.

Stoicism understands that the past cannot be brought back. Those facts happened. It's not like you can jump into a time machine and go back and change those facts. That's just simply not going to happen. You just have to deal with the consequences of those facts, right here, right now.

Similarly, stoicism enables people to get over worrying themselves silly over things that have not yet happened. There are so many people out there that are so fearful of things that can go wrong. These are people who are so worried about how things will happen in the future. Talk about wasted energy.

Those things have yet to happen. They have yet to play out. But here you are, wasting a tremendous amount of your focus and emotional energy worrying about things that could happen.

Interestingly enough, stoicism teaches that the more skilled you are in handling the present moment and controlling it to the best of your abilities based on your emotions and your decision-making powers, the greater you can control your future. It all boils down to focusing on what you can control.

The past is the past, and it's water under the bridge. The future has yet to happen. The only thing that we have power over is the present moment. This includes our feelings, our emotions, our perceptions, assumptions and expectations.

Believe it or not, by taking control over these and understanding how they flow into each other, we end up making better choices, which leads to a brighter and better tomorrow. At the very least, it leads to less pain, humiliation, embarrassment, disappointment and frustration.

This is practical stoicism. Instead of focusing on changing the world, you focus on changing yourself from a deep and fundamental level.

Chapter 2: Why Should You Become a Stoic?

What are the benefits to being a stoic? How can this ancient philosophy benefit you in the 21st century? What are the practical implications of a stoic life?

There are at least 8 ways stoicism can benefit you. Please keep in mind that this list is a partial list. It is by no means a comprehensive list of all the possible benefits you can get from this philosophy. Still, I've distilled and summarized a huge amount of related benefits into these 8 major benefits.

Benefit #1: You take control of your emotions

Believe it or not, people screw up their lives, not because they planned to. I've yet to meet somebody that actively seeks to screw up his or her life.

Instead, they just find themselves acting impulsively at certain moments in their lives. It often takes one bad decision for your life to make a 180 degree turn and head towards your worst nightmares.

Oftentimes, that change, as drastic as it may be, happens because people let their emotions get the better of them. It's as if they see and hear something and all of a sudden they go into autopilot mode and they end up saying, thinking and doing the worst things.

Believe it or not, the world doesn't really care about your feelings. What it cares about are the things you do. Once you start to act a certain way, the world sits up and pays attention and rewards and punishes you accordingly.

If you do not get a firm handle on your emotions, it should not surprise you that you end up reacting in the worst way possible once you are triggered. This is no way to live an effective life.

If you look at truly effective and successful people, they have found a way to respond positively to certain situations in their lives instead of letting their emotions get the better of them. Conversely, great biographies of people who have hit the peak only to fall from grace often involves scenes where they let their emotions take over.

Benefit #2: Stoicism enables you to form better relationships

By taking fuller control over your emotional states and your perception of reality, you are able to take a step back from your selfish impulses. Instead of automatically assuming that all life is about you and you alone, you get access to tools that enable you to take a step back.

When you're able to do this, you will be able to empathize more with other people. You will be able to see yourself in other people.

Life doesn't have to be all about you. Everything going on in your life doesn't have to involve drama that is important to you. Instead, you can see glimmers of yourself in other people, and this enables you to develop better relationships. You listen better, and you actually seek to understand.
Instead of trying to dominate other people or impose your will on them, you quickly

discover that they are worthy of respect. You quickly understand that they have interests that are worth protecting.

Ultimately, you discover the value of other people. They are not just means to an end. Instead, they are ends in and of themselves.

Benefit #3: You learn how to make more rational decisions

According to a recent psychological report on decision-making, researchers discovered that most Americans make decisions on impulse. When asked to explain their decisions, they then come up with rational sounding reasons.

However, in the spur of the moment, their decisions were actually impulsive. They based their decision on their emotions in the heat of the moment.

Unfortunately, rash or impulsive decisions usually don't lead you to optimal results. Often times, they end up making your situation worse, or you put you in a bad situation.

You make all these impulsive, emotional decisions based on what you're feeling at that moment and you end up saying the wrong things to the wrong people at the wrong time to produce the wrong consequences.

You can lose jobs. You can basically disqualify yourself from future promotions. You can harm your relationships. You can make yourself less healthy because you can't resist food. The list is endless.

It all boils down to impulse. Impulse is usually not rational. Impulse usually arises from emotions.

Stoicism enables you to make decisions based on reason. This means that you are going to be basing your decisions on the values that you yourself have consciously selected. You won't be basing your decisions based on how you feel at any given moment.

Benefit #4: You overcome your natural greediness

Let's get one thing clear, the natural state of the human mind is to ask "What's in it for me?" It's all about I, me, mine. If you think that this does not apply to you, think again.

If you scratch deep enough below the surface, you would understand that the way most people look at the world is through the fixed lens of self. Stoicism enables you to work within this framework so that your approach to the world enables you to be victorious. It really does.

If we were to always focus on ourselves first and we let our natural greediness and selfishness take over, we end up developing an entitlement mindset. We become softer and weaker.

We start thinking that the world is unfair just because it did not roll over the moment we showed up. We think that there is something fundamentally wrong with other people and systems that run the world because we did not get the respect we feel is due us just because we showed up.

When you shift your focus from selfishness and greed to how the world actually operates, you overcome that sense of entitlement. You start operating your life based on how the world actually operates instead of how you wish it operated.

Benefit #5: You will be able to overcome procrastination

One of the biggest problems people struggle with when it comes to productivity is procrastination. We keep thinking that there will always be a tomorrow. Not surprisingly, we feel that we can run away from the big projects or the big things that we need to confront in the here and now.

When we get the idea in our heads that there will always be an infinite supply of tomorrow, we all too eagerly kick the can down the road. Instead of confronting the big things that hold you back and drag you down from the success that you are otherwise capable of achieving, you stop doing that.

Instead, stoicism enables you to live in the present and appreciate your power in the present moment. Since it re-centers your mind to your ability to focus and devote your physical, mental and psychological resources to what's in front of you, it trains you to procrastinate less. It trains you to take care of what can be taken care of right here, right now.

This doesn't happen overnight. But the more you do this, the cleaner your to-do lists become. Sooner or later, your big goals start getting done. If you keep this up long enough, you end up becoming more successful than when you began. Funny how that works, right?

Instead of stressing out over the important stuff that you know you need to do right here and now, you focus less on stress. Instead, you focus more on getting stuff done. It's all about empowerment in the present moment.

Benefit #6: You get out from under social pressures

What if I told you that the vast majority of people out there who are struggling with finding contentment are stuck in that position voluntarily? That's right, they cannot find fulfillment because somehow, some way, they have bought into the idea that they will only be happy if they please other people. They feel that they will only be "somebody" if they meet somebody else's definitions or somebody else's expectations.

Adult kids do this all the time when it comes to their parents. It's not unusual for children to enter professions that they, dep down inside, hate just because they're trying to please their parents.

The worst part to all of this is that they end up resenting the people they feel put them there. They are so afraid of letting people down. They are so afraid of disappointing others that they would rather turn their lives into a personal hell.

Stoicism enables you to get out from under that social pressure. Instead, it teaches you the right mind frame to start living your life for yourself.

Interestingly enough, the more you do this, the more respect you command from others.

The more you do this, the healthier your relationships become. This is one of the most paradoxical benefits of stoicism.

Benefit #7: You learn to truly prioritize

Did you know that 80% of the things you do every single day only account for 20% of your results? It turns out that a very small fraction of your daily activities, say 20%, actually produce 80% of your results.

Whether we're talking about income, productivity, social contacts, it doesn't matter. This principle, called the Pareto Principle, applies across the board. In fact, it applies to groups of people as well.

Did you know that 20% of any population group owns 50-80% of all the wealth in that group? The same applies to sports teams. Did you know that 20% or less of the typical NBA team accounts for 80% or more of the points scored by that team?

Understanding this universal human principle and applying it to how you do things on a day to day basis can truly liberate you. It really does. Because you are able to work less, yet earn more or produce more. Wouldn't that be awesome?

Stoicism gives you the frame of mind that enables you to think more efficiently because you are trained to live in the present moment. You are trained to look at what you are focusing on and see which produces better results.

You are able to connect the dots better. You are able to see patterns that lead to better results. Eventually, you reach a point where you are able to get more results with as little inputs as possible.

Of course, this doesn't happen overnight, but it begins with the personal resolution to focus on life on a day to day basis.

Benefit #8: You learn to be truly honest

The essence of stoicism is to focus on the things you can control. This is the bedrock of this philosophy. It is its foundation. Implicit in this is a deep and profound honesty.

It's really going to be very hard to live your life fully in the present moment and tap all your personal assets and potential if you are telling fairy tales to yourself. If you are delusional, nothing will happen.

Accordingly, stoicism pushes you to be as brutally honest about yourself as possible. Instead of telling yourself the fairy tale that you have an IQ of 140 or 160, you are pushed to realistically deal with your intellect and work from there.

It's really hard to build stuff if you are under the delusion that you have a lot more resources or tools than you actually have. Building that amazing new building is simply not going to happen because you don't have the equipment or the materials for it. That's just out of the realm of possibility.

After struggling through these enough times, stoicism wears down your all too human tendency to tell yourself stories.

Another key aspect of the human condition is self aggrandizement. We tell ourselves stories that puff ourselves up. We consider this as part of human pride. We end up over exaggerating and overestimating our capabilities.

But when you practice stoicism, you chip away at that. Instead, you look at reality. You look at the foundations of your life. Instead of crying over the fact that you're not as smart, good looking or physically fit or good with money as you believed yourself to be, stoicism considers this sobering discovery as a good thing.

By clearing away the fluff and looking at the foundations of your life with unvarnished eyes, stoicism celebrates because now, you know what you're working with. Now, you know your foundations. It may not be much, but at least you now know what you have to work with and, most importantly, what you can build on.

Stoicism is crucial if you want to live a more effective life. It is very simple. In many cases, it's very elegant, yet it's extremely powerful.

By focusing on the world the way it truly is instead of imagining it to be something that it's not, stoicism gives us the tools to live truly meaningful and fulfilled lives.

Now, this doesn't mean that you're going to be happy all the time. This doesn't mean that you're always going to come out on top, but it's definitely going to mean that you're going to experience something better than the life of quiet desperation and frustration that you have now.

See you in Chapter 3.

Chapter 3: Ten Steps to Practical Stoicism

What follows is a quick list of the ten steps you need to follow to practice stoicism on a day to day basis. A lot of people think that stoicism is this vast, grand philosophical system that needs special preparation. In fact, some people are under the impression that only a few select, very intelligent and sophisticated individuals would truly understand stoicism.

Others truly believe that stoicism is too complex. It may be great in terms of theory and abstraction, but completely impractical when it comes to day to day living. All of these ideas are absolutely wrong. You can practice stoicism on a day to day basis. You don't have to be a spiritual person, have a philosophical bent nor be some sort of intellectual. If you're just the regular everyday Joe from middle America, you can still practice stoicism and, most importantly, benefit from it. Here are the ten practical steps to stoicism that this book will teach you:

Step #1: Do a practice negative visualization

Step #2: Analyze your personal situations using a personal "control grid"

Step #3: Start and maintain your very own philosophical journal

Step #4: Seek out and impose discomfort on yourself

Step #5: Practice defining your personal boundaries

Step #6: Meditate or practice mindfulness regularly

Step #7: Identify and write down your life's purpose and re-read it regularly

Step #8: Practice giving

Step #9: Enroll in some sort of physical or endurance training program

Step #10: Keep studying stoicism

What follows are in-depth discussions of each step. Each chapter would have examples of the specific step in action. It will also mention scientific studies that support the effectiveness of the step being discussed.

Chapter 4: Practice negative visualization

Think of the worst things that can happen in certain areas of your life. For example, at work, think of the worst thing that can happen as far as your work performance, as well as relationship with others. In your relationships, think about what could possibly go wrong. With your health, think about the worst thing that could happen to you. Imagine all of these things and allow yourself to be prepared for them.

Always think to yourself, if the worst things in the world happen to me right here, right now, will I be ready for them? Preparing for the worst case scenario does not just involve the right kind of insurance. Making sure that you are properly insured against all sorts of exposures is definitely responsible and is required. You're being responsible and mature when you do that, but you have to do something more. You also have to be mentally and emotionally prepared for the worst things that could happen.

The best way to do this is to spend some time by yourself and go through a list of your worst case scenarios. Close your eyes and visualize yourself going through these experiences. Allow yourself to visualize in three dimensions. Don't just focus on the things that you imagine seeing. Instead, pay attention to the things that you will hear, touch, taste and smell. The more senses you engage in this "visualization" of the worst case scenarios in your life, the more emotionally engaged you become.

You lock in to certain emotional responses that you would go through. This enables you to control your emotions, while you visualize. This is how you prepare. In the beginning, if you're completely honest with yourself, you'd probably freak out and would be running around like a chicken with its head cut off. But as you go through these negative visualization experiences again and again, you start zeroing in on the proper emotional and psychological state. Again, this is not easy nor is it natural.

But the more you practice, the more you will know what to do. If bad things do happen in your life, since you have mentally and emotionally prepared yourself for the worst, you would be able to handle them in a calm, responsible, mature and adult manner. Instead of letting your emotions take over and simply reacting, you are able to calmly handle situations, so they at least don't become worse. At best, you might even be able to turn what would otherwise be a tragedy into an opportunity for gain or learning.

Examples of this step in action

Example #1

Imagine yourself losing all the things you own. Imagine yourself walking into your apartment or your home and everything is gone. You just got cleaned out. How would you feel? What is the worst thing that could happen after that happens? Can you see any opportunities? Can you imagine recovering from that loss. Once you played this scenario over and over again, you start detaching yourself from worldly wealth. You would start discovering the fact that your wealth does not define you. You would start learning that your material possessions don't indicate your value as a human being. You start developing a mental and emotional distance from your possessions. You would also learn how to store your insurance policies the right ways, so if you get cleaned out, you would at least be able to recover by making an insurance claim. There is a practical aspect to this. In addition to being robbed, you might also want to consider imagining losing your possessions to some sort of fire or natural disaster.

Example #2

Imagine yourself getting really sick. Imagine yourself catching a really messed up disease. Maybe a stage four cancer or some sort of communicable disease. Imagine yourself going through the process of being stuck in bed and thinking about the very real possibility that you're going to die.

When you go through this process, you learn how to accept the limits of your life. You begin to understand all too well that you are mortal. You come face to face with your physical vulnerability. The practical benefit of this is that you start to think about getting life insurance or some sort of asset protection for people who will survive you. On a deeper emotional level, you start practicing becoming at peace with your own mortality and vulnerability. This way, when you get sick and you are incapacitated for a long period of time, you take it in stride. You stop thinking of it as the end of the world. You stop overreacting. Instead, you have emotionally trained yourself to see things in perspective and to recover later on.

Example #3

Imagine yourself losing the most precious person in your life. Whether you have a child, a spouse, a significant other, a parent, imagine losing that person. This is the person that you value the most in life. Imagine yourself going through the loss. Imagine the pain, the sense of being alone and feeling abandoned. Go through these emotional hoops, exaggerate them and get used to them. When you do this, you learn to develop emotional balance if and when the unthinkable happens. We live in an imperfect world. A lot of the people that we value the most in life can easily die. They can be taken away or go away, whatever the case may be. We cannot allow ourselves to become emotionally tied to them to the point that we become emotional cripples when they disappear from our lives.

Go through this exercise so you gain some sort of mental and emotional distance. This doesn't mean that you stop valuing them. Instead, you actually get know their full value, but you also prepare yourself to let them go. Either because life is so uncertain that there may be situations where you will be taken away from them or they will pass away. Whatever the case may be, be emotionally and mentally ready for that possibility.

Example #4:

Imagine if you're a slave. Imagine yourself in prison. Imagine yourself in some sort of physical or legal situation where you cannot do what you want to do. Imagine that you were stuck doing something that you hate for eight hours a day. Whatever the case may be, imagine yourself in a situation where you really do not have any control over the things you do, as well as the physical things in your life. When you do this, two things happen. First, you appreciate your freedom. Oftentimes, we only appreciate what we have when it's gone. There's just so many things that we take for granted. We only miss them when they're gone.

For example, you only realize the value of having a healthy kidney when you develop kidney stones. When you're struggling in pain, that's when you realize that you had healthy kidneys before, now you don't. You were taking your kidneys for granted all this time.

Most of us are guilty of taking our freedom for granted. Did you know that there are millions of people all over the world that cannot go where they want to go, do what they want to do because they're in jail. They're in prison. In fact, in many places in the world, people are slaves. In this day and age, there is still de facto slavery.

Another benefit that you get from this exercise is you learn to try to make the best of a bad situation. If you do find yourself in prison, what would you do? Would you mope around and say that life is unfair and that you are a victim of some injustice? Are you going to keep banging the rails of your jail cell hoping that somehow, someway people would sit up and pay attention to you? Or would you do something productive? Imagining yourself in a prison cell, totally forgotten by the world, can be a very depressing situation. But if you keep picking apart that scenario, you can start coming up with solutions. Maybe you would read, write stories, try to learn some sort of trade or engage in some correspondence training. Maybe you would welcome spiritual missionaries or evangelist. Whatever the case may be, find yourself completely stuck and try to figure out how you can achieve freedom, even when you are not physically free to leave.

Example #5

Imagine being dismembered. Imagine your limbs being torn off or losing sense of sight or hearing. When you do this, you appreciate your body, your physical capacity, your ability and whatever health you have. Most people spend 24 hours in a day taking for granted a lot of the blessings that they have. The fact that you have two eyes that can see is a massive blessing. The fact that you can hear, move your arms and move things around, we don't appreciate these until they're gone. This mental exercise enables you to appreciate your body and, most importantly, prepare your mind and your emotions should you lose these capabilities. Imagine yourself being totally paralyzed. In the beginning, it would be a very distressing experience and seem like you've lost all hope because you cannot move. The more you practice this negative visualization, the more you would realize that even if your body has completely shut down, like the famous astrophysicist, Stephen Hawking, your mind can still be free and imagine beautiful possibilities.

The "counterclockwise" study by Ellen Langer indicates that the way you think impacts your health and mind

In 1979, Ellen Langer, a Harvard psychologist, published research that showed that when people imagine themselves at a different age range, they perform differently. This actually had a direct impact on their health. Similarly, when you practice negative visualization, the mental and physical preparation you engage in, influences the actual physical state of your health and mind. In a University of Washington paper, published by Scott Freeman, a biologist, students who are in the wrong emotional state failed to absorb the lessons of lectures.

Freeman's research indicated that there is a direct connection between the mental focus of students and their ability to absorb alternative information. In other words, our mindset indicates our ability to absorb any kind of alternative information. This is significant to negative visualization because if you adopt the right emotional state when you are imagining all sorts of alternative realities, their implications sink deeper into your consciousness and you are more likely to learn from them. This paves the way for actual changes in your behavior.

Similarly, in a study on weight lifting, scientist discovered that people who imagine themselves lifting weights were more likely to develop positive physical changes. This happened before they even lifted a single kilo. In other words, in terms of negative visualization, when you devote a tremendous amount of mental focus on alternative realities, you are more likely to benefit physically, as well as do well when you actually start on these plans.

Chapter 5: Analyze your personal situations using your personal "control grid"

When you're dealing with some sort of issue, always think of the situation in terms of what you can control and what you can't. Focus on the aspects of the situation that you can control. Usually, this means our emotional response. In many cases, that's the only thing we can control because everything else is completely random.

A good example of this is your home being hit by an earthquake or a hurricane. You obviously can't control the weather, but you can control your response. You may think that it's the end of the world, then you just sit there all paralyzed and devastated emotionally, unable to do much of anything or you can choose to respond in a different way. You can choose to think that this is not the end of the world and you only need to find your insurance paperwork to start the long process of getting your life back on track. You can always choose your response.

You are completely in control of your response.

Example #1

When your flight is delayed due to bad weather, please understand that you can't waste your time thinking about the weather. As much as you can try, your mind won't make the clouds go away. Your mental focus won't make the tornado disappear. That's just not going to happen. Instead, you can control what you choose to spend your time on while you're waiting for your flight to become available. When you do this, your mind doesn't focus on things you can't control. This prevents you from being frustrated and angry, pointing the finger and trying to blame factors that you really cannot help. Instead, you can just simply whip out a mobile phone, type out some email, check out updates on Facebook, download some game apps or do something else that would take your mind from the things you cannot control to the things that you can control. You can control your use of your time.

Example #2

When you're faced with a tremendous amount of stress, you cannot control the physical effect it has on you. You still grit your teeth and want to tear your hair. But you can control how you cope with it. You know that if you cope with it a certain way, you're going to exhibit certain physical symptoms. So you can look at more productive ways to deal with stress. Maybe you can take a walk or do some deep breathing. You cannot control the direct physical effect of stress if you let it fester.

However, even you control how you cope with it, you indirectly control its physical effect on you. You less likely to stew in anger and frustration when you're walking around the block. At least some of your physical energy is being diverted. Understand that you always have this option. You can't just take stress lying down. You can choose to cope with it in a variety of ways.

Example #3

When you get injured, you may not be able to control the pain, but you can control how you handle the pain. If you stub your toe, there's really nothing you can do. The pain will happen and is automatic. What you can control is how you deal with the pain once it appears. You can take Tylenol or get an ice pack and wrap it on your toe. You can take off your shoe, put your foot on a footstool and massage your foot. Instead of obsessing about the pain, cursing it and getting upset, focus on making the pain go away. At the very least, you save yourself from developing infection and making things worst.

Example #4

When faced with an upset significant other, understand that you cannot control your partner's emotions. He or she is going through a tough time handling what you or she just said. You cannot control how they would respond, but you can always control how you react to their response. Understand that you can blow up the drama level or be a source of soothing words and relaxing emotional signals so your partner can calm down. Sure, they may be completely unreasonable in their reaction, but if you choose to call them out on that and explain to them how unreasonable they are, you're not really helping the situation. If anything, you're going to be making it worse.

Since you know you can control how you respond to their overreaction, then you have to wear the adult pants in the relationship. You would have to step up and be the mature voice of reason, at least, for today. The key is to dissipate conflict and foster real communication, either right now or later on. Your objective should not be to point out who's wrong and who's right.

Example #5

If you're in a class and your teacher simply doesn't know how to teach, you obviously cannot control their teaching style. However, you can control how much effort you put into looking through the materials your teacher gave you and figure things out. Avoid the temptation of blaming your inability to learn on your teacher. They may be teaching in a very incomprehensible way, but that does not absolve you of your responsibility to figure out the lessons based on the materials they've given you. Two teachers, working with the same book can produce totally different results. One person simply cannot teach his way out of a wet paper bag. There are teachers like that.

There are, however, other teachers, who can take whatever information they need to teach and present it in plain English that people can readily absorb. If you're not lucky enough to get the second type of teacher, then you still have to wake up to the responsibility of learning from the materials supplied by the teacher. You have to take ownership. Don't be all too eager to point the finger at the teacher who cannot teach. At the end of the day, it's still your responsibility to learn.

During the American Psychological Association's 122nd annual convention, a researcher, Wendy Wood, presented her findings that concluded that individuals experience certain mental habitual patterns that enable them to assert fuller control, regardless of whatever situations they get into. These are habitual patterns that people develop, even when they're dealing with situations outside of their control. By simply falling into these patterns, they are able to either turn things around or at least minimize the damage. These are chosen patterns that we can learn.

According to KC Chesterton from the University of Cambridge, while stress is unavoidable, we can control how our neurons respond to the things stress brings with it. For example, when you experience stress, usually anxiety or depression is soon to follow. In the Chesterton study, simply taking action on whatever project assigned to you is much better than procrastination. When you choose to procrastinate, the stress produces anxiety. You feel more and more powerless. Eventually, you feel stuck. So you put things off again and again and again. According to Chesterton's research, by simply focusing on what you can control, which is the decision to take action on the task that you've been putting off, you actually diffuse the anxiety that stress brings to the table.

In 2007, researcher, Olivia Remes, from the University of Cambridge, concluded that even if people go through really trying times, they can still choose to do certain things that would end up benefiting them. As an example, Remes told the story of a person in a coffee shop when it begins to rain. This person is in the interior space of the coffee shop when it begins to pour. She wants to go home, but she's stuck. It's raining outside.

According to Remes' study, stress dissipates even in really trying times, when you choose to focus on something you have control over. In her example, instead of stressing out and freaking out about the fact that she was stuck inside the cafe because it's pouring cats and dogs outside, she simply reached into her backpack, took out a homework assignment and started doing it. By shifting our focus of control, we can actually benefit from really tough situations. It may well turn out that the person in Remes' story may not have gotten around to doing her homework if not for the fact that she was stuck in that cafe during a downpour. Always remember that you have at least some area of control in any situation you find yourself in.

Chapter 6: Start and maintain your philosophical journal

Unlike your regular journal, your philosophical journal is where you write down things that happen during the day. You write down what happened to you and you also analyze how you responded to these situations. You note down how you reacted to people's input, as well as how you viewed situations. By doing so, you become aware of your mental and emotional patterns. You start seeing problem areas, but you also start seeing areas where you can take full control. This can pave the way for you developing certain habits that would enable you to practice more personal control, regardless of what's happening and your external circumstances. By writing this down, you can see your progress. You can also analyze things that you may have completely overlooked, if you did not write them down.

Example #1

In your journal, write down what happened during your day and how certain events led to certain reactions. When you do this, you will be able to create a tighter connection between the things that you see, hear, touch, taste, smell and how you feel or think. The more you do this, the tighter the connection becomes. You start connecting the dots and seeing certain patterns. If you're able to do this, then you would be able to start predicting how you would respond. You only need to see certain things happen for you to start predicting that you will respond the certain way. If you're able to do this, then you can start changing your reactions.

Example #2

Note down whether your reactions were optimal or not. Only you know whether your reactions to certain triggers during the day were positive or negative. Of course, to pull this off, you have to be completely honest with yourself. When you do this, you will be able to identify areas for improvement. You will also be able to gauge the effectiveness of your responses. Keep at this long enough and you will be able to identify other ways you could have responded which could have led to better results. Of course, you shouldn't just write this down, you should also practice alternative reactions the next time certain things or certain situations happen. Keep repeating this process and switching your responses until you get to the most optimal response.

Example #3

Note in your journal your perception of progress. Usually, when you look at the first day of your journal and compare it to the most recent day, you should see some sort of change. This might not be a black and white change, but when you compare those two different dates, you should be able to see some small changes, how you size up situations and what kind of options you see for yourself. This would enable you to gauge the progress of your journey and teach you to pay close attention to certain factors and warn you to stop certain patterns. At the very least, you will be able to stop doing things that hold you back and drag you down from maturing as a person and build on the things that are working.

Example #4

Note the times when you are angry or stressed. When you note the times that you got upset, two things happen. First, you get a clear idea of what triggers you. It may seem like you just stepped in a roller coaster and there's not much you can do once you get into that train of thought or once you start feeling certain emotions. Don't worry about the lack of control, instead focus on the tight connection between the trigger and your emotional state. Another thing that happens is that you are able to get some sense of relief when you let your emotional hair down. Just pour it out. The worst thing that you can do is to deny that certain things make you angry.

For example, if you have issues with your father or things that your father or mother did in the past, it doesn't really help you when you keep lying to yourself that you don't feel upset about those memories. You have to be completely honest with yourself. Nobody's going to read your journal unless you give them access. This is just for you.

By understanding the direct tie between certain memories, certain physical triggers or events that play out in the here and now and certain emotional states, you start on the road to progress. Because you know that certain things trigger you, you then start looking for ways to cope and diffuse that connection. Is there any other way you can respond or read these negative memories, so they're not as negative?

Believe it or not, some people are able to think about the same negative mental images, but respond in such a way that those mental images no longer have their sting. That's how you get to the path of self-healing. Unfortunately, none of these will happen if you do not write this stuff down and you do not practice complete and total honesty when chronicling this material.

Example #5

Document any realizations you have about your practice of stoicism. Stoicism enables you to be self-aware. However, it doesn't operate automatically. You have to be self-aware at all times that you are practicing stoic techniques. When you document how you consciously shifted your emotional response from the predictable and all too usual negative response to something neutral or better yet positive, you will make progress. You have to be aware that you're practicing stoicism and of your options. By documenting this, everything becomes clear to you. Eventually, you will be able to make the right decisions more frequently. This enables you to take fuller and fuller control of your life. It also enables you to see your progress as you practice stoicism.

In a University of Texas study, released in 2013 by researcher, James Pennebaker, simply writing down one's personal experience in a journal enables people to emotionally recover from any kind of hurt

People are able to start on the road to healing by simply writing down their experiences. The journal that you are keeping for this step is more thorough than just simply writing down your experiences. Since you are properly mapping triggers and your responses to them, your chances of overcoming negative patterns are much higher with the self-awareness stoicism teaches you.

According to a 2007 research study from Birmingham, involving people in support groups who have lost loved ones, simply keeping a day to day journal, helped 80% of the study's participants to achieve some form of closure. They started to heal better because they wrote down their impressions. They were able to forgive themselves and move on. The lead researcher for this study was a mother who lost her young son in a car accident. She was driving the car and was having a tough time forgiving herself because her son died.

In a University of California study led by Professor Lieberman, 20 volunteers were tasked to keep a journal. For days, they were supposed to just write down their experiences for at least 20 minutes. At the end of the journal phase, the study participants had several measurements taken of their brain functions. It turned out that those who wrote extensively about their emotional experiences, showed greater activity in the right side of their prefrontal cortex. This is the part of the brain that is most closely related to the relaxed state of minds. Individuals who poured out their emotions through their journals were reported feeling happier and more relaxed because they were able to let go of their mental focus in certain experiences. It simply did not bother them as much.

Chapter 7: Intentionally Impose Discomfort on Yourself Regularly

For this step, you're going to purposely subject yourself to some sort of physical or emotional discomfort. When you do this, you train yourself to take less things for granted. It also enables you to prepare yourself physically, mentally and emotionally for uncomfortable times.

You have to understand that people who can't handle tough times set themselves up to fail. They always seek comfort. They always insist on the very best conditions.

When those conditions are impossible to get, they become very fragile. They start crashing like a house of cards at the smallest discomfort. It doesn't take much to throw them off track.

When you purposely subject yourself to all sorts of discomfort, you toughen up your skin. You are able to handle all sorts of situations. You also become mindful of the things that you normally take for granted.

You become aware that a lot of things have to fall into place for you to live comfortably. You never lose sight of that because when you purposely subject yourself to discomfort, you deny yourself of creature comforts. You become aware of just how blessed you are as a person.

Regardless of how much money you make, regardless of which part of town you live, and regardless of your status in life, you focus on what you have and the great things you have going for you.

Unfortunately, most people would only become aware of these things when they are taken away. You, on the other hand, purposely take these away from yourself to remind you of what you have and also to prepare you for times where you have to live without.

Example #1: Fast regularly

When you let go of food for at least one day on a regular basis, you not only toughen yourself up mentally and emotionally to physical deprivation, you also access a tremendous amount of health benefits.

Did you know that human growth hormone can be activated by fasting? Did you know that you can trigger your body's fat burning capabilities when you go on a fast? In fact, according to research studies, people who regularly go on fasts extend their life span. Ironic, right?

Example #2: Dress lightly when going out in the middle of winter

When you purposefully underdress when going out during winter time, you toughen yourself up to prepare yourself for situations where you won't have access to a coat or won't be comfortably warm. Your mind will be ready for these situations. You may be able to reach a point where you can say to yourself, "been there, done that."

Additionally, when you do this, you practice empathy because you will be able to imagine how cold homeless people get in the middle of winter. This enables you to become more empathetic or compassionate person.

Example #3: Purposely close your eyes and try to walk around

Now, I don't recommend doing this out in traffic. You might be putting yourself in harm's way. But within a fairly controlled area, allow yourself to walk around with your eyes closed.

When you do this, you subject yourself to fright, stress and anxiety. You appreciate the fact that you have eyesight. You appreciate the fact that you can see depth.

You also prepare yourself for the unthinkable. If something happens and you lose your sense of sight, you won't get (pardon the pun) blindsided, either physically or emotionally.

Example #4: Intentionally stop using your hands for a whole day

For a complete 24-hour period, refrain from using your hands while getting around. When you do this, you appreciate your limbs and your hands. It also enables you to understand what you're taking for granted. It also jogs your creativity and imagination.

If you cannot use your hands, but you still need to pick stuff up, you better think quickly. You start becoming more resourceful. Practice this enough and you would be able to get out of sticky situations if your mobility or ability to move things around were seriously limited.

Example #5: Intentionally turn off the power in your home

Now, you may be thinking that when you turn off the main switch to your home that, at worst, things will just go dark. Boy, are you in for a surprise. You may not be aware of it now, but when you turn off the power, your refrigeration shuts down.

If you live in a particularly warm part of Western Europe or the United States, you would quickly realize the value of your fridge.

You would also train yourself to store food in a more strategic way.

A lot of people who are preparing for disasters intentionally pack only dry goods. These are goods that only need warm water to prepare. Some food actually don't even need water to be eaten. You start thinking along those lines.

When a disaster strikes and you have practiced turning off power to your home enough times, you probably would be able to overcome such challenges.

In a 2013 study by the University of Pennsylvania Wharton Business School, in partnership with the Harvard Business School, study participants were deprived of certain amenities. The study reports that people who had a lot of common amenities taken away from them were more likely to express gratitude.

Many of these participants indicated that, by being deprived of things that they usually take for granted, they started to change how they looked at their lives and how they value their daily lives.

Similarly, in a report coming out of the University of North Carolina at Chapel Hill, researcher Sara B. Algoe stated in 2014 that being separated from her significant other made her feel more thankful for the relationship she had.

By intentionally staying away from each other during the experiment, she became more appreciative of the romantic connection she had with her partner. This led to an improvement in how she was able to relate to and understand him.

In a 2012 study conducted by Doctor Martin Seligman from the University of Pennsylvania, several participants were asked to answer questions without thinking of the answer. They were asked to answer quickly.

Predictably, all participants failed. When they were given the opportunity to think about what just happened, many participants started to appreciate how their psychology worked and how their brain functions.

Seligman concluded that this experiment showed that when people are psychologically deprived of their thinking processes, people stop and appreciate the fact that they are able to engage in such processes.

All of these scientific studies lead back to the fact that stoicism's intentional deprivation of certain experiences help us become more aware. We become more grateful. We also are able to prepare better for certain situations in the future.

We don't set ourselves up for instant discomfort. Instead, by toughening our skin, we will be able to better handle whatever life throws our way.

Chapter 8: Redefine Your Personal Boundaries Regularly

When you define your boundaries, you spell out the things that you will spend your time on and which things you will spend less time on. Stoicists practice this to maximize their sense of control over certain areas of their life.

You are fully capable of choosing certain parts of your life that you are going to spend more time and focus on and intentionally cutting out or cutting down other parts of your life. The more you do this, the more control you have on your life. You don't end up living your life basically at the mercy of the people around you.

You see this happen a lot at work. You're doing your thing and your buddy comes up to you and asks you to do something, and then soon enough your boss tells you to do something. At the end of the day, you weren't able to do much of your own work. You then repeat the same pattern day after day, week after week, month after month.

When you practice boundary definition, you are able to focus your attention on only certain tasks, and this enables you to work more efficiently. This also enables you to master certain areas of your life.

Now, keep in mind that this mastery doesn't have to remain restricted in those areas. You can actually expand your areas of expertise.

Example #1: Evaluate which relationships foster your well-being and focus on those

When you do this, you are able to cultivate relationships that help you blossom as a person. You also distance yourself from toxic people in your life. These are emotionally needy people. These are people who take up a lot of your time without really adding much value to your life.

Now, you don't necessarily have to cut out these people, but you can take control over the negative impact they have on your time and life.

On the other hand, by focusing on people who help foster your well-being, either through encouragement, mental and emotional support, or even physical support, you enrich your relationships.

You end up giving them more of what they're looking for and strengthening your relationship. They are already doing you a big favor, but when you focus on them, you're returning the favor.

Example #2: Evaluate the jobs that you do every single day and focus on return on effort

When you define your boundaries in terms of your daily work practices, you start identifying things that you do every single day that really don't add much value to your life.

Take your work, for example. In the span of an 8-hour period, you're probably spending a lot of time doing email. Chances are quite high that replying to email is not exactly what you're getting paid for.

Can you imagine doing less email and doing more of what you are being paid to do? Not only does this increase the likelihood that you may get promoted or get a raise, but it would also help you become a more productive person.

Example #3: Evaluate the things that you condone

There are many things that you let slide every single day. These are things that you basically just automatically accept. You may not be all that comfortable with them, they may not necessarily make you happy, but you just let them slide.

Start saying "no." Or at the very least, start analyzing before walking away. The more you do this, the more effective you become.

You start training more of your time and focus on the things that add more value to your life. You also start pushing away toxic people who suck out a lot more resources than they contribute.

Do this for a long enough period of time and you may retake certain core areas of your personal life. You may have ignored these for a long time, but it would be amazing once you recognize that, for the longest time, you've actually been letting people leech off you.

Example #4: Evaluate daily activities that burn up a tremendous amount of your willpower

When you line up the daily activities that actually take a lot of decision-making effort from you, you would quickly realize that a lot of them are really inconsequential. Imagine having to spend more than 10 minutes trying to figure out which coat or tie to wear. Imagine worrying yourself silly trying to figure out which cologne to use.

Interestingly enough, highly effective managers keep wearing the same clothes because they know that their willpower is precious. They'd rather focus this very scarce resource on things that truly matter.

For a great example of this, you don't need to look any further than Steve Jobs. There's a reason why Steve Jobs keeps wearing the same black turtleneck. Believe me, it's not because he can't afford other pieces of clothing. The guy, after all, was a billionaire.

The reason why he used the same turtleneck and blue jeans outfit day after day is because he'd rather focus his willpower on stuff that truly matters, like the next design of the Mac or the next generation of iPhones.

Do the same. There are many decisions in your life that burn up a tremendous amount of willpower, but really don't change your life all that much. Focus on what truly counts. Focus on what will push the ball forward.

Example #5: Evaluate which daily tasks you enjoy the most

Come up with a grid where you look at the things that you enjoy the most and the value that they produce. See if you can find activities that you truly enjoy, but which also provide the best return for your time, effort and focus. Do more of these.

If you do these, your boss will start to notice. If you do this, you will become more productive. If you keep at it, the quality of your work improves and you become an expert in certain areas of knowledge. It's only a matter of time.

When you're driven by passion, you become more and more competent and you become more and more valuable.

On the other hand, when you look at work as this giant burrito of tasks that you have to eat at one sitting, you don't really become a master of anything. Instead, you're just running around in circles trying to put out fires. Not exactly a winning strategy for a successful career.

In 2014, researcher Adam Bandt released a study that, based on logistics, most citizens usually don't contribute much to the organizations that they are part of. Bandt identified the activities and the amount of time involved.

Apparently, the average person could not go longer than ten minutes without checking their phone or mobile device. And, interestingly enough, the vast majority of the time they spend on their mobile device involves pretty much worthless activity like watching porn.

This highlights the fact that unless you actively define your boundaries to focus on things that add value to your life, it's too easy to get stuck in an activity pattern. That doesn't really move your life forward.

Sure, you're doing something habitually every day. Sure, you're engaging in some sort of activity, but if that activity doesn't really add value to your work or your personal life, you're just chasing your tail. You're just wasting your time. So regardless of how many times you check your phone, this does not necessarily improve your productivity.

In another research study released in 1996, Santa Monica Schools of London teacher Hannah Houston reported that kids who spent more of their time studying at home performed better at tests than kids who spend most of their time watching TV or playing video games.

Now, this might seem like common sense, but this study highlights the fact that what you focus on impacts your personal productivity. When you spend your time studying, you are able to perform better at academic tasks.

But if you spend the same amount of time doing things that don't prepare you for academic tasks, you don't do all that well. This is regardless of how naturally talented you are.

It doesn't matter what your IQ is, if you don't practice because you don't have the right focus and you haven't defined your boundaries properly, you're not setting yourself up for peak performance.

I know this sounds obvious, but we need to look at the science to see that this is the case. A little bit of focus on the right things does go a long way.

Similarly, in a 1964 study released by psychologist Wandy Ham, people were interviewed regarding their relationship with their families, friends and romantic partners.

According to Ham's study, people who intentionally surrounded themselves with positive individuals were in a better situation in life. Not only were they mentally and physically healthier, but they were doing better financially and socially.

This study highlights the fact that when you analyze your social connections and you redefine your boundaries, you get different results. You don't just take whatever life throws your way. You just don't take the random people that you normally attract throughout the course of the years.

Instead, when you draw boundaries as to the people you're going to spend more time with and invest your emotional energy on, you are treated to a positive return on investment because you're more careful.

Stoicism teaches you to define your boundaries in such a way that you position yourself for better results. That's the bottom line.

Chapter 9: Practice Regular Meditation and Mindfulness

The ... ions regarding
mec ... are under the
imp ... rt of mystical
esca ... s idea in their
hea ... now some sort
of r...

Hmm... maybe you and I can do this in early mornings before school & work?

None of this correct. When you meditate or practice mindfulness, you're only doing one thing and one thing alone: you are focusing on the present moment.

When you do that, you quiet your mind. You focus your mind in such a way that it relaxes and it expands. You refresh your mind's natural capability to experience reality. As a result, you re-energize your mental faculties.

This is a very important and strategic investment in your life. When you're able to do this, you are less likely to let your emotions get the better of you because you are able to see things in perspective. You tend to develop a larger mental picture of what you're up against, and this helps you avoid freaking out unnecessarily.

Example #1: Practice morning meditation and reflection on things that can go wrong and the ideal way to respond to these

Instead of practicing regular meditation where you watch your breath or you hold your breath for a few seconds, and then you let go, and then hold your breath again, focus on your imagination. Think about the things that could possibly go wrong in your life, but refuse to react emotionally. Instead, just pretend you are watching a movie in a very dispassionate way, but really bad things are happening in the movie.

Now, imagine yourself looking at yourself as you watch the movie. I know this sounds weird, but it's very empowering. Imagine yourself being that third party observer of you watching the movie, coaching yourself to effectively respond to the scenes that you're watching in the movie.

By approaching your experience this way in a meditative state, you are reprogramming yourself on so many levels. Psychologically, you are teaching yourself to look at things in perspective. On an emotional level, you are teaching yourself to be more sanguine in your reactions. This enables you to anticipate things that may happen in your day and respond in the most optimal way possible.

Example #2: Practice exercise meditation

A lot of people are under the impression that meditation simply means assuming the lotus position and then just zoning out. No, that's not true. You can meditate while you're moving your body.

Did you know that yoga is a form of meditation? Practice yoga and relax and unwind while engaging in physical exercise.

Believe it or not, you can tone your muscle mass while practicing yoga. If you need proof of this, just look at Madonna and how she was able to get toned by simply practicing low impact yoga.

The great thing about yoga is that you not only exercise your body, but you're also exercising your mind and personal focus at the same time. There are, of course, many flavors of yoga, so try to focus on the more secular ones.

Example #3: Practice stress meditation

Stress meditation simply means taking time off in a very deliberate way from your schedule. Basically, you just let go of everything for a fixed block of time.

Maybe this is two hours per day or maybe four hours per week. Whatever the case may be, you just zone out for that block of time.

It's important to make sure that you are in a place where you're not going to get stressed and you are not going to be disturbed. You're just going to train yourself to do absolutely nothing for that block of time.

I have to admit that when I first did this, it was very uncomfortable because my mind kept trying to think of certain things to do.

But the more you do this, the more you let go of stress. You unclench your personal and essential core and you become incapable of stressing out.

It really is a beautiful thing. However, it takes quite a bit of time and practice.

Example #4: Practice gratitude meditation

After you have achieved a relaxed state of mind, maybe after you have counted your breath or you have visualized certain relaxing scenes, focus on things that you're grateful for.

Focus on things that you feel thankful for, like the fact that you eat three square meals a day, you've got great friends, you have a supportive family, and you have a great home. Whatever the case may be, consciously and proactively think of the great things you have going for yourself.

Allow that sense of gratitude to bubble up from deep within you. Zero in on the mental image and try to move yourself to the point of tears that you are so thankful that you have these things in your life. When you do this, you train yourself to be grateful for your complete life.

For example, when you train yourself to meditate on the gratitude you have for the fact that you have a job, you start being thankful for your boss. Sooner or later, you start being thankful for the things that you normally are not all that comfortable with as far as your job is concerned.

This applies across the board. This applies to your relationships, your home, your health, and so on and so forth.

This sense of gratitude relaxes you. The drama in your life starts to dissipate. You start seeing the big picture. You start seeing things in perspective.

Example #5: View your world from above

In this meditation style, imagine yourself looking at your world from above.

Start at five feet above. You look at yourself, your immediate environment, and then imagine yourself going up in altitude to a hundred feet. Imagine what you'd see. And then go up to 1,000 feet, then 10,000, then 100,000, then 100,000 miles, and on and on it goes.

When you do this, it starts to dawn on you that your daily drama, disappointments, frustrations and anxieties are not big deals. You start seeing yourself in the big scheme of things.

You start realizing that when you have a big enough perspective and you are dealing with a long enough timeline, none of this really matters. And instead of feeling diminished, depressed or discouraged, this actually can help you feel really good.

Because prior to this point, you've been beating yourself up over all these crises that have been breaking out throughout your life. You start realizing that, at the end of the day, this stress doesn't really matter. Instead, you open yourself to the possibility that gratitude will replace stress in your life.

In a series of research studies conducted in the 1970s centering around the University of Massachusetts' stress reduction clinic and center for mindfulness in medicine, Professor Zinn discovered that a lot of study participants, mainly students, felt sick. They were not physically sick. Their sickness symptoms can be traced to stress.

Zinn switched some of the study participants from stress reducing medication to meditation. The results were just nothing short of amazing. These individuals were able to get rid of their stress by simply relaxing their minds.

This cognitive research paved the way to many other academic and institutional research on the wide range of benefits meditation and mindfulness bring to the table.

In a Harvard Business School study released in 2001, researcher Sandra Coublon concluded that entrepreneurs and business people who regularly meditated or practiced mindfulness tended to do better in business.

The big difference? Participants who meditated and actually kept a journal regarding their daily activities tended to do better. The increased focus paired with keeping journals and books, tended to take these entrepreneurs' performance to a much higher level.

In a 2012 seminar conducted by David Hanks, fitness instructor based in California, he reported that clients of his who practiced yoga tended to be more fit. Compared to people who did not practice yoga, people who practiced yoga tended to be more organized. They also tended to look younger because they lost wrinkles and fine lines. Plus, they tended to be leaner.

All these studies highlight the fact that when you practice meditation and mindfulness, you are taking control of your mental processes.

When you do that, you are able to take control of your emotional state, which enables you to make better decisions. At the very least, you are able to plan out your actions in a more orderly way so you can enjoy more predictable and more positive results.

Chapter 10: Write Down Your Life's Purpose and Read It Regularly

Did y ... ife has a constit ... s and most other ... ion. This is the le ... e operations of the

This might be easier said than done, but I think it'll give you focus.

Believe it or not, constitutions mean a lot. Badly written constitutions often lead to bad governance. Constitutions that enshrine bad economic or governance systems tend to foster corruption, inefficiencies and waste. Funny how much of an impact a set of written codes may have on the collective behavior of a country.

Well, if constitutions have this impact on a macro level, can you imagine how a written personal life purpose may impact people on a micro level?

Stoicism teaches us that when we identify and actively select and define our life purpose, we take greater control over our lives.

Now, a lot of people would find this corny or downright cheesy. It's easy to see why a lot of people have this attitude because if you worked for any kind of company in the United States, chances are, that organization has some sort of mission or vision statement.

When was the last time you actively looked at your company's mission and vision statement? I would wager to guess very rarely, if that.

People usually don't take this type of stuff seriously. In the back of their minds, they have better things to do. I really can't blame them. But you have to understand that the more intentional you are as far as your life purpose is concerned, the more control you have over your life.

Think of it as writing a script for your life. You're not writing a line by line screenplay for your life where your every decision is mapped out in advance. Instead, you are riding the general plot lines for your life. This is much better than just taking shots in the dark and hoping for the best.

When you have some sort of well selected and well planned master script for your life, you can tell yourself where to go and this can help guide you in making decisions. You are more likely to make decisions based on your highest ideals and values instead of simply giving in to your emotions. This increases the likelihood that you will achieve the life that you want for yourself.

Example #1: Think of your personal purpose in relation to your career path

How well aligned is your career to your life purpose? Maybe a lot of your frustration with your work stems from the fact that it doesn't line up with the kind of life ideals you would like for yourself.

In this situation, you either have to quit your job and find something that is more consistent with your life ideals, or you're going to have to find meaning in what you're currently doing for a living. Something has to give.

Example #2: Think of your purpose in relation to your life partner

If you're in a relationship, pay attention to what's going on in your relationship. Pay attention to the power balance in your relationship.

This is not just a matter of being happy or content. Instead, look at the big picture of your relationship. Do you feel like you are being validated as a human being in that relationship in the same way as you'd like to be validated by your life purpose?

Again, just like with our choice of career, if there is some sort of disconnect, it's time to make some adjustments. Either you pick a better partner or you start making changes in your relationships so that it lines up with the highest values you have selected for yourself.

Now, unlike your career, this is a little bit trickier. In this situation, you are dealing with your romantic partner. This means that you have to respect their decisions as well.

So any changes must be neutral. Otherwise, you may be putting so much stress on your relationship because you're trying to align in with your personal values that your partner feels that the relationship has become imbalanced.

Again, something has to give. If they feel that that imbalance is just too strong, they may walk. It has to be mutual. You have to let them know what's going on. You have to also pay attention to their life ideals.

Often times, relationships are actually third parties. They are not simply reflections of what you want or what your partner wants. Instead, the relationship itself has its own agenda. It has become a third party and both of you have to give something up for that relationship to blossom and grow.

Example #3: Think of your personal purpose in light of the people you surround yourself with

Now that you have a clear idea of what your life purpose is, is this lining up with your social life? Do you surround yourself with people who share the same values? Do you see yourself in a group of people that share the same general direction?

Now, this doesn't necessarily mean that everybody has to be the same. This doesn't necessarily mean that everybody has to agree on the same general values and general goals. However, the people that you surround yourself with must at least be supportive.

It's okay to differ. It's okay to have different values. After all, opposites attract. There is, after all, strength in diversity.

But if you notice that you are surrounding yourself with people who are toxic and who are always telling you that you cannot do things or even telling you that your values are wrong, you might want to take a step back. You might want to slow things down and ask yourself whether you should establish some distance with these people.

Again, this doesn't mean that you have to cut them out. You just have to properly realign them so they don't get in the way of your life values and your life purpose.

Example #4: Think of your life purpose in relation to your relationship with money

Everybody has a relationship with money. Whether we admit it or not, we have a relationship with money. Some people, believe it or not, are scared of money. That's why money never comes near them.

Ask yourself, "Does my life purpose line up with how I look at and pursue money?" If there is a disconnect, then you need to change your attitude towards money. If your life purpose is to be financially comfortable, but you are scared of taking risks, there's going to be a problem.

Accumulating capital is, by itself, risky. There is always a chance of loss. As the old saying goes, no pain, no gain.

If you are sick to death of the possibility that you are going to lose money when you invest it, then your conception of yourself retiring very financially comfortable needs to change.

Either that or you need to change the way you look at risk and accumulating money.

Example #5: Think of your purpose in relation to major life decisions

As I have mentioned above, no pain, no gain. Put in another way, if you're not willing to risk anything, don't be surprised if you don't gain much of anything.

Believe or not, the world works in terms of risk. Your ability to drastically improve your life is actually joined at the hip with your ability to undertake risks. They go hand in hand. The more risks you take, the higher the chance you will gain great rewards.

Keep this mind when looking at the relationship between your personal purpose and major life decisions like moving. A lot of Americans are scared to death of moving. Maybe they grew up in a certain city or state. They just cannot accept the fact that if they want to move up in terms of income, career trajectory or quality of life, they have to move.

You have to stop being scared of this. You have to look at it straight in the eye. Is your life purpose and your desired ultimate life outcome lining up with your attitude towards making life decisions? This really all boils down to your willingness to sacrifice.

In a 2003 research study out of Oxford University, Professor E.L. John concluded that when study participants thought about their life purpose, they tended to save themselves from making big mistakes.

Not surprisingly, the same study discovered that students who had an idea of what their purpose for studying certain classes or courses were, tended to do better than students who basically just made random choices as far as their courses were concerned. A little bit of purposefulness can go a long way as far as your life's results go.

Similarly, the University of Pennsylvania's Sandra Ham released in 2000 a study that says students who simply wrote down their personal purpose tended to be more successful than those who didn't.

Finally, in a Harvard study release in 2013, Teresa Amabile studied 30 subjects. Among the subjects who wrote down what their life purpose was tended to make better progress with their studies. How come? They tended to be more principled in how they went about things.

Stoicism teaches that when we identify our purpose and stick to the tight parameters of our purpose, we give ourselves meaning. We tend to make less mistakes. We also tend to be more efficient as far as our actions are concerned. This leads to more purposeful action, which leads to greater results.

A little bit of purpose, as I've mentioned above, goes a long way. Stoicists have known about this for hundreds upon hundreds of years.

Chapter 11: Practice Philanthropy

Believe it or not, you don't have to be a multimillionaire to be a philanthropist. I know this sounds shocking because the popular image of philanthropists are people who set up multi-million dollar foundations.

To be a philanthropist, you have to rediscover the Greek meaning of the word "philanthropy." "Anthropos" means man, "philos" means love. To be a genuine philanthropist, all you need to do is to genuinely care for other human beings.

You just have to genuinely have some level of love for your fellow humans. That's all philanthropy boils down to. And yes, you can cultivate philanthropy, even if you don't have much cash.

In this chapter, I'm going to teach you how stoicists can cultivate this sense of seeking others. Paradoxically enough, the more you seek others and try to help and fulfill them, the more you feel fulfilled.

Example #1: Think of your friends as family and treat them as such

When you tell your friends that they are family and you actually follow through, the relationship becomes deeper. It enables you to step out of your deep and profound sense of selfishness. Everybody starts out from this point.

When we were babies, we were extremely selfish, but it's the mark of maturity when we outgrow that point and we actually start caring for other people. We start looking at other people, not so much based on what we can get out of them, but based on how much we can give them. This is the true mark of maturity.

When you tell your friends that they are family and you start treating them as such, you start making progress with this transition.

Example #2: Volunteer in a home for the aged or for orphans

It's very hard to practice real compassion when you are simply being good to people who are good to you in return. It's hard to practice real compassion when there is something in return; when you are nice to somebody who you know has the capability to be nice back to you.

You really are taking your personal philanthropy to a whole other level when you practice kindness to people who cannot return the favor. When you volunteer for a home for the aged or you spend time helping orphans, you practice real selflessness.

Because in many of these cases, these people will take, take, take and take. They will stretch your patience to the breaking point, and this is precisely the point. That's when you realize whether you are just simply going through the motions or you're making progress in your intentional effort to become more selfless.

Again, it's easy to be compassionate when you are dealing with friends and family members. You love them, and they love you back. It's hard to practice compassion to people who take, take and take and never say "thank you." That's when you know you are being a real philanthropist.

Also, when you volunteer in a home for the elderly, you also become aware of your personal mortality and the reality of aging. This enables you to step out of the mental fiction that most people suffer from.

Most of us, although we're not willing to admit it, operate from the assumption that we will remain youthful enough. In fact, some people are under the impression, again a lot of this is subconscious, that they will remain young forever. When you surround yourself with aging, you see this reality eye to eye and you break out of that mental fiction.

Example #3: Counsel people

Among people you know as well as among people you come across, never be stingy with advice. Even though you may not have money, you can still help people out with advice.

Now, you may be thinking, "Who am I to give advice? I'm not some sort of expert." Well, you may be surprised as to what you know because just by simply living your life, you develop expertise. At the very least, you have seen certain things that people might want to learn from. People might want to hear what you have to say, and that might benefit them.

Don't think that just because you don't have an official title of psychiatrist, psychologist, or licensed clinical social worker, that you can't give people advice. Even in your times of failure like failed relationships, failed businesses or personal depression, you can gain useful experiences that can help other people.

When you allow yourself to counsel people, you give them a helping hand. You step out of yourself. You start training yourself to think that the world is not about you. That it doesn't have to revolve around you, your needs, your issues, your drama. That it's perfectly okay to open up and be about other people.

Example #4: Visit rehab centers and jails

It's easy to love lovable people. It really is. In fact, in many cases, a lot of people develop a habit of loving people 90% knowing full well that people will give them 95% back. They become some sort of emotional banker.

These are some of the games that we play with ourselves if we're not careful. Well, if you find yourself thinking along those lines, you can quickly destroy such comforts by going to jails and drug rehab centers and engaging in counseling. You will then start to stare life in the face.

Life is not always pretty, manicured and well kept. Life sometimes has bad breath. Life sometimes curses you to your face. Life is sometimes rude, obnoxious and even threatening.

But when you stare life in the face the way it is, on a completely real level, you start to grow up. You start to realize that you have all sorts of assumptions on how people should be; of how people should react when they're being helped or when people are being kind to them.

When you start seeing the full gamut and range of emotional interaction with other fellow human beings, you pop your cherry. You really do. You let go of the self serving fictions that you have.

You learn how to give, give and give when all the person on the other end seems to focus on is to take, take and take. And worst of all, they forget to say "thank you." In fact, in many cases, they even spit at you. That's when you know you're making real progress.

Of course, you shouldn't take any of this to mean that you should put yourself in harm's way. But when you allow yourself to become psychologically thrown off center by other people's reaction, you start to poke holes at that comforting emotional cocoon you have about emotional reciprocity.

When you do that, you mature as a human being. How? You start to love and appreciate people regardless of the fact that they cannot emotionally reciprocate. You start to love people even though the only thing they can repay you with is hate, condemnation, judgment, mockery, ridicule.

Example #5: Strike up a conversation with a total stranger

Now, this is kind of tri [illegible]
remember that they have [illegible]
uncomfortable. Unfortun[illegible]
ways to get around this.

You may be technically talking to a stranger, but if this person looks like you, talks like you, comes from the same educational background as you, has the same goals as you, has the same values as you, and he may even have the certain types of friends that you have, you're not really talking to a stranger. You're talking to somebody who looks more like a mirror.

If you really want to break out of your emotional cocoon, you need to talk with a total stranger. This person has to look different from you, has to come from a different class background, different educational background, has a different attitude from you. We're talking a 180 degree difference.

How do you know you're successful? Very simple. You're scared. The moment you feel fear is the moment that you know you are talking with a total unknown.

Take full advantage of this opportunity. Truly listen to them. As different as they are, try to put yourself in their shoes.

Don't try to impose your judgment on them. Don't try to cram your solutions down their throats. Instead, open your heart and truly listen.

Now, this doesn't mean that you have to love them. This doesn't mean that you have to wish you were them. Instead, this exercise is all about connection. When you go beyond the outer limits of your fear to break through and actually make a connection, that's when you know you're actually maturing.

In a study by a neuro-scientist out of the London Frances Crick Institute, he studies how people interacted with each other, and he had identified that there are two types of people who can help others. There are people who can help people in need directly. These are people with the right advice or the right expertise.

However, there is also another group of people who are very, very much needed. These are people who may not be able to help directly because of their lack of expertise, but they know somebody or they know somebody who knows somebody.

By mapping out these social interactions, the neuro-scientist Ben Martynoga helped redefine the different types of philanthropists.

In a graduation interview conducted in 2011 by Yale University Professor F.D. Jake, the professor concluded, in all his interviews of high level philanthropists, that they pretty much all have one thing in common. They all feel relief and peace when they touch someone's life.

When stoicists practice philanthropy at any level, they escape the gravitational pull of their ego. This enables them to connect with people on a deeper level.

Most importantly, it enables them to connect with themselves at a deeper level and really prioritize what matters. It also helps them to truly connect with people regardless of whether these other individuals have anything in common with them.

Philanthropy is one of the best things you can do as a stoicist because it enables you to see the social world in full context. Usually, people see their social world in terms of its relationship to their own ego. It's as if they're looking at other people with these sunglasses that communicate their personal truths, which other people may not value or may not believe in.

Chapter 12: Sign Up for Some Sort of Physical Training

Stoicists make it a point to sign up for some sort of physical training where their physical limits are pushed. This doesn't have to be extreme. You don't have to necessarily sign up for some sort of MMA training program. Just by signing up for self-defense, martial arts, you can go a long way in handling discomfort.

You also learn discipline. Most importantly, you learn how to overcome setbacks. Make no mistake, if you engage in any kind of martial art or sports training, and you compete, most of the time you will lose. That's just a fact of life unless your name is Michael Jordan or LeBron James or Stephen Curry. If you engage in basketball, there's a good chance that you will lose. Not just once, not just twice but again and again and again.

This gives you a tremendous opportunity to learn how to deal with setbacks and most importantly how to learn from failures. Signing up for any kind of physical endurance or physical training, trains both your body and your mind. You start to align your mental, psychological and physical discipline together. In fact, with the highest level of training, you end up punishing your body which in turn frees your mind. Believe it or not, the more physical strain your body can handle, the stronger your mind becomes. You eventually reach the point where you conclude that your physical comfort doesn't set limits to your mental strength and emotional focus.

Example # 1: Take up martial arts

Any kind of martial arts, whether we're talking about taekwondo, judo, karate, you name it! Teach yourself control and most importantly learning to take instructions in a physical setting. There's one thing to learn from a teacher in a purely intellectual setting. For example, if your high school teacher is teaching you geometric concepts, it's very easy to let things slide. Concepts go in one ear and concepts go out the other ear.

It's hard to do this when you are learning martial arts because if you don't listen carefully, you might go down. You might get hit. You might get hurt. You might get harmed. This enables you to open your mind to learn in a wider context. This can then help you to learn in a regular educational context.

Example # 2: Swim continuous laps

The great thing about swimming is that it's a low impact type of exercise. The more you swim, the more you increase your endurance. The great thing about swimming is that you can level in a fairly low impact way. Compare leveling up at swimming with leveling up with weight training. There is no comparison because when you try to level up doing weights, your muscles will feel it. In fact, if you do it wrong, you will feel sore for quite a long time. Not so with swimming. Still, when you practice continuous laps, you push yourself to the limit and this enables you to build endurance. This is a crucial part of practical stoicism because if you let yourself stay within your comfort zone, the walls of your comfort zones or the outer boundaries of what you feel you can and cannot do start behaving like prison walls. You start allowing yourself to become comfortable within this zone.

What would you think would happen? If you don't constantly push against them, they start caving in on you. Sooner or later, you're not capable of doing much because almost every little bit of effort is too much. Keep pushing against your comfort zones by increasing your endurance through sports or any other kind of cardiovascular activity.

Example # 3: Run long distances

The great thing about long distance running is that you don't necessarily have to run at a very high level of speed. You can actually jog at a fairly low level speed. What's important is that you are able to put out effort at a consistent pace over a long period of time. A little bit of consistency goes a long way.
Another great advantage of jogging long distances is that you're able to meditate on your life. Consider it an active form of meditation not much different from yoga. You start thinking about the things that you are doing. You start drawing some connections. Sometimes you connect the dots

and you see patterns. Whatever the case maybe, when you are constantly putting out physical effort over an extended period of time to cover long distances, things starts falling into place in your mind. You start seeing the big picture. It's no surprise that a lot of business leaders tend to come up with their best ideas when they are engaged in some sort of long term physical activity like jogging.

There is a strong connection between physical activity and emotional catharsis. According to the self-proclaimed greatest of all time boxer, Muhammad Ali, he said that when he was younger, he would often go boxing when he was feeling upset. The more he boxed, the more the anger, pain and disappointment would subside. Instead of acting out their negative emotional state, practical stoicists would rather engage in physical activity that would burn up negative emotional energy in the form of physical energy. Again, a little bit of physical exercise could go a long way.

Another example of this is the story of Tyra Banks, the host of America's Next Top Model.

Banks shared in 2012 the fact that physical exercise helps models become more productive. When they are engaged in physical exercise, a lot of the daily stress involved in the model lifestyle goes away. They're able to handle a lot more responsibilities and become more productive.

Similarly, if you are dealing with any kind of emotional stress, try to let off steam by simply working out. This is a great way to get a handle on your emotions in a very positive way. Best of all, not only are you managing your emotions, you're also physically exercising. Not only do you feel better, but you can also start looking better.

Chapter 13: Actively Study and Analyze Stoicism

By studying the lives of famous stoics and reading stoic philosophy, you get to immerse yourself in this school of thought. It's one thing to engage in practical stoicism but you need to also ground yourself in the philosophy. Interestingly enough, the more you physically live out some of these stoic principles, the deeper the meaning you get from stoic literature.

Example # 1: Read stoic books and articles

When you read a lot of online articles on stoicism, you learn how to filter information very quickly. As you can well imagine, the internet is chock-full of all sorts of information. When it comes to stoicism, there's a tremendous amount of information available online. Not only does reading up on a tremendous amount of stoic literature help you get a better understanding of what this philosophy is all about, it also trains your mind. If you're exposing yourself to a tremendous amount of information, you quickly learn how to sort information. You quickly learn how to detect patterns and assess value. This enables you to become a more effective researcher and a more discriminating reader. At the end of the day, you become a more student.

Example # 2: Take notes on what you learn

People who simply read one book and one article after another are actually letting a lot of very important information fall between the cracks. If you don't believe me, pay attention to this pattern. Keep reading the same article over and over again or keep watching the same video over and over again. You should come to the realization that after several amounts of viewing the same video or reading the same article, you discover certain facts that you didn't "see" before. Now they've been there all along but the problem is you took you several exposures to that article or video for you to become aware of that information. This is why casual reading can only help you to a certain extent. You have to take notes on what you read.

There's the right way to take notes and the wrong way to do it. The wrong way to do it is to simply take notes while you're reading. This is how you take notes in class. Usually, you don't do all that well when you do this because at the back of your mind, you think that you've done a good job figuring out what the item is and you don't have to consult with your notes. You develop a sense of complacency. The best way to do this is to read the material or watch the video and then, in your own words, explain it to yourself and ask little words as possible.

When you do this, you force yourself to remember what you just witnessed and prioritize what is important. You then go through the materials again to double check and this enables you to connect the dots and come up with a richer appreciation which can then summarize in a few lines of notes. Believe it or not, these notes tend to stick and they tend to have a more positive impact on how you actually do things and how you think.

Example # 3: Take specific courses in stoicism

Casual study can definitely be helpful. But let's get real here. When you study any kind of subject matter on a casual and purely voluntary or optional basis, you really have no skin in the game. You're really not giving anything up. You're definitely not sacrificing anything of value. Instead, you are just getting around to doing it when you have time to do it. For some people, this works well. But let me tell you, for the vast majority of people, this is a flat out disaster because let's face it, life gets in the way. You may have the very best laid plans in the world but life has a terrible habit of getting in the way. That's just something that is more pressing or higher priority and you simply don't get a run to doing it. Not surprisingly, your understanding of stoicism remains incomplete.

The way to override this is to tap the power is commitment. When you actually put yourself in a situation where you're going to have to give up some cash, that's when things get real. When you start feeling the financial pain, you start paying attention and you can commit. When you commit, you are able to learn in a structured way which leads you to absorb more and more information. This increases the likelihood of whatever you learned sticks around for quite some time. Stoicism is so powerful you really cannot mess around with it. You have to learn it the right way so it can have a deep and profound impact on your life. This requires commitment.

Take courses on stoicism online. Pay the membership fee. The higher the fee, the better because this enables you to have skin in the game and it focuses your attention because there's some sense of loss. You're paying good money for this course, so you better learn it.

Example # 4: Join a stoicism discussion group

When you a discussion group around stoicism, you learn from people who are fellow students. You compare notes. You encourage each other. You share each other's joy. You also excite each other regarding the facts that you may have stumbled upon. Whatever the case may be, by going through a process together, you are able to share and learn from each other. Oftentimes, the best way to learn something is to teach it to others. When you join a stoicism discussion group, you get a tremendous opportunity to teach others what you know.

What really takes things to a whole other level as far as your personal education is concerned, is your willingness to be corrected. If you are humble enough to be corrected, then discussion groups will be a tremendous blessing to you. You will be able to learn but if you think you're always right, then you might want to think twice. You might want to let go of that attitude because you might actually be creating more problems than you are solving by joining a discussion group.

In terms of actual research regarding stoicism, work produced by Richard Lazarus and Folkman centering around the Goodness of Fit Hypothesis or GOFH. In 1984, it shed some light on how stoicism works in a clinical setting. The idea is that when we focus on healthy coping mechanisms, we're able to function better. A key component of this is the sense of control that we feel when we are confronted with the problems of everyday life.

There are many different components to this and a lot of this leads to CBT or Cognitive Behavioral Therapy. CBT is a very respected form of therapy and can help people overcome fear, anxieties and certain types of depression. Practicing stoicism and learning more about it positions you to increase your sense of control over your life which can help position you for a more effective life.

Conclusion

This book teaches you the key steps in practicing stoicism on an everyday basis. We try to stay away from the mysticism, or philosophical talk surrounding stoicism. Instead, we ground the information in practical psychology and scientific research. The ball is in your court. You know what to do. These steps are well drawn out. They are not overly complicated. They are actually simplified so you can start on them right away. You have to understand that when it comes to any kind of practical information that can possibly take your life to a higher level, you need to supply one crucial ingredient. Without this ingredient, all the amazing information in the world is not going to change your life one bit. That's simply not going to happen. What is this missing ingredient? Commitment!

It's not enough for you to take action on great information. You can take action one day and completely drop the ball for the rest of the year. That's not going to help you. Similarly, you cannot just work on something and then work on it every once in a while. You have to stick to it day after day, month after month, year after year. It's all about commitment. The good news is that you don't have to be a hero. You don't have to jump in with both feet and come in with both barrels blazing. You don't have to do that. It doesn't have to be a high intensity kind of experience. After all, baby steps forward are still steps forward. Regardless of how small your initial steps may be, as long as you are moving forward, you are making progress. I wish you nothing but the greatest success!

I thought this book would be cooler... oh, well Merry Christmass habibi anyway ♡

DISCLAIMER

While all attempts have been made to verify the information provided in this publication, the author does not assume any responsibility for errors, omissions, or contrary interpretations of the subject matter herein.

The views expressed are those of the author alone and should not be taken as expert instruction or commands. The reader is responsible for his or her own actions.

The author makes no representations or warranties with respect to the accuracy or completeness of the contents of this work and specifically disclaims all warranties, including without limitation warranties of fitness for a particular purpose. No warranty may be created or extended by sales or promotional materials. The advice and recipes contained herein may not be suitable for everyone. This work is sold with the understanding that the author is not engaged in rendering medical, legal or other professional advice or services. If professional assistance is required, the services of a competent professional person should be sought. The author shall not be liable for damages arising here from. The fact that an individual, organization of website is referred to in this work as a citation and/or potential source of further information does not mean that the author endorses the information the individual, organization to website may provide or recommendations they/it may make. Further, readers should be aware that Internet websites listed in this work might have changed or disappeared between when this work was written and when it is read.

Adherence to all applicable laws and regulations, including international, federal, state, and local governing professional licensing, business practices, advertising, and all other aspects of doing business in any jurisdiction in the world is the sole responsibility of the purchaser or reader.